SWIPEABLE

Avoid The 8 Mistakes Men Make On Dating Apps
& Discover What Women Actually Want

CAMILA ARGUELLO

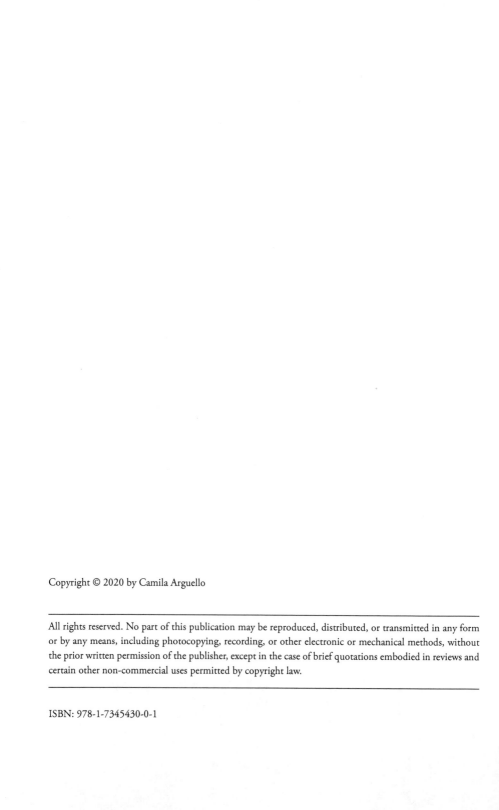

ISBN: 978-1-7345430-0-1

To those who inspired it,
may you one day find it

CONTENTS

Download the workbook free!

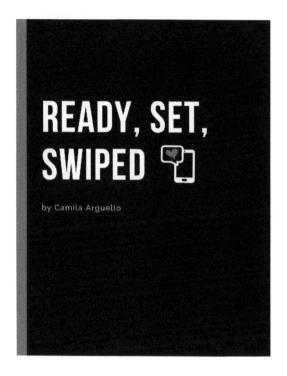

Read this first

I put together a workbook of all the action steps inside *Swipeable* to help you take immediate action on upleveling your online dating presence. It's FREE for you as a thank you for buying my book.

To download go to:
https://camilaarrinudo.com/workbook

« INTRO »

It started as a joke. Before that though, it began as a bet. I'd been dumped by the same guy for the third time in a row and I knew that after we met to talk about getting back together, it was going to be the last time. I was done.

Two weeks later, I was ready to look elsewhere and ready to try some creative solutions. I was sitting in the car with my sister when I asked if she'd heard about "that Tinder thing?"

We looked at each other, and then simultaneously jumped onto the app store. We didn't really know what we were getting into. To our surprise, "that Tinder thing" wasn't just a single app, but a whole list of options all promising one thing: a better dating experience. After scrolling through, my sister proposed a bet to see who could get a date from one of the apps the fastest. I wanted to have fun and meet new people after the drawn-out breakup I'd just had, so I laughed and then agreed. She decided to try OkCupid while I downloaded Tinder and off into the world of online dating we went. I remember laughing with her over dinner as we showed each other some of the profiles we stumbled across and the conversations we were having.

To be honest, I don't remember who won the bet. What I do remember is that after that night, Tinder became my go-to boredom reliever. It took a month of swiping to meet someone decent. We met and ended up dating for a year before things ended. Since I'd enjoyed it before, I jumped back into the Tinder world with gusto. Around the same time, I decided I liked having company in the endeavor and convinced a friend of mine to let me download it onto her phone. I even offered to write her profile because, let's be honest, she wasn't going to be good at it. As her friend, I had to give her an honest shot online, and I figured why not? After setting up Nicole's profile, I started wondering about all the other apps I'd seen in the App Store. I am nothing if not a woman who wants options, so after further investigating, I discovered that there were a truly overwhelming amount of dating apps. I dove in. For the next two years, I downloaded every app that sounded interesting and tested them. Tinder, Bumble, Hinge, OkCupid, Plenty of Fish, Coffee Meets Bagel, Clover, Happn....if it's a dating app, there's a good chance I tried it at some point.

At first, I was interested in the apps and their functionality. I looked at which interfaces were easier to use than others, what differentiated the different platforms, the different demographics on each, etc. Eventually, I became curious about the industry the apps existed in so I read articles about online dating and later fell in love with *Modern Romance* by Aziz Ansari and Eric Klinenberg. Changes in romance due to technology became one of my favorite topics to discuss (much to the chagrin of my roommates). About a year and a half after I started testing apps for my own personal use and researching online dating, I was tasked with selecting a topic for a semester-long project for one of my college classes about media. I jokingly sent in a proposal for investigating Tinder, and to my surprise, my professor approved it. Thus began my academic passion for the topic. While working on the project, I found an entire section of fiverr.com where freelancers offered services for online dating gigs and decided to post a profile editing gig of my own, for research purposes. At this point, I'd been rewriting friends' profiles for a couple years and found it fun, so I thought I should finally be paid for it. When I got that first order, it lit up a passion which hasn't dimmed since.

When I started getting paid for rewriting profiles and analyzing pictures, I quickly saw a distinct difference in demand. While I had edited profiles for many friends, both female and male, my clients were almost exclusively men seeking women. It became clear more men were struggling to create profiles which appealed to the opposite sex so I started asking women what they thought about Tinder. Some women loved it, others hated it, but the complaints I heard about men's profiles were all pretty similar. It's been a few years since that initial order and to my surprise, regardless of a woman's age, the complaints have stayed pretty consistent.

Let's be honest, with the cloud of hookup culture and social stigma still lingering around dating apps, there's plenty of statistics, and yet little concrete how-to info out there. I love working with men and improving their dating lives through their online presence, but I also recognize that not every man will seek out help to begin with. And so, this handbook was born.

What you're holding is the product of five years worth of personal experience, app testing, 60+ completed profile overhauls for clients, and countless conversations with men and women about their experiences in the online dating world. My mission with this handbook is simple: to help your profile go from sucky to swipeable and help you gain confidence. You're a successful guy, so why bother having a shitty online dating profile? Maybe you've tried apps in the past and have given up because they just didn't work, maybe you're frustrated because you're getting matches but not dates, maybe you haven't even downloaded an app because it seems like a waste of time. Wherever you're at, I want to meet you there.

Ready?

A NOTE FOR THE SKEPTIC

You might be thinking there's no way you'll ever get on Tinder. (I would then wonder why you bought this book in the first place.) "Who even wants to meet someone on the internet? That's so cliche," you might say. But the fact of the matter is, today, around 40% of couples in the US met online[1]. Beyond that, more than a third of marriages are between partners who met online[2]. So clearly it's working for some people. Not to mention, it might just be one of the most practical tools for romance you have available. You're able to use it when you want in the comfort of your own space. Dating apps offer control and the ability to direct a lot of your dating life. I'm not saying you can't meet someone at a bar, the grocery store, or through mutual friends but you have this in your hands and you're still looking, so why not give it a shot?

PART I

YOUR APPS

CHAPTER 1

IT'S NOT YOU, IT'S THE APP.

Mistake: You're on the wrong app.

I'm going to let you in on a secret: most men mess up their chances of success on dating apps before they even set up their profiles.

Why? They're on the wrong one. The first thing you have to know about online dating is that every app is *not* the same. Picking the right one from the get go can save you a lot of time and potentially, money too. If you're confused here, don't worry, you're definitely not alone. A lot of people make the mistake of thinking that getting on any app is the same. After all, it's the internet, so there should be no difference, right? Wrong. I think that this happens because people view dating apps by their stereotypes rather than what they're individually designed for. People know eHarmony because of their cheesy TV commercials, Tinder has a reputation for one night stands, and Farmers Only, well, speaks for itself.

There are two reasons why choosing the right app is vital. First, straightforward and simple is always better. It's better to have a killer, simple Tinder profile than a shit OkCupid profile because the latter requires answering more questions and therefore, more effort. So if you slack off and half ass it, there goes half of your results too. I'll talk about it more later on, but each app requires different information so picking the right app from the beginning can save you a ton of effort in the long run.

Secondly, if you've never spent money on a dating app or service, you're probably wondering how saving money by picking the right app makes sense. You may not necessarily think of this when you first start, but let's say later down the line you want to invest in some of the *paid* premium features. It would be better to do it on the app you know fits your needs rather than paying for six months of useless features before realizing you should've been on a different app all along.

One of the frustrations I've often seen with men that have dating apps is that often, the problems they're trying to correct using premium features are problems they could've avoided in the first place if they picked the right app from the start. Sure, $10 might not seem like a lot at first glance, but do you really want to be doing the equivalent of lighting a $100 bill on fire every year?

Now that I've burned the importance of being on the right platform into your consciousness, here are some things to keep in mind when thinking about the right app(s) to pick:

What do you want to get out of the app? Meaning, did you download an app so you can swipe every night, get a boost of confidence as you get matches and sleep well knowing that women out in the world find you attractive? I would hope you don't need an app to feel self-worth, however for the purposes of this example, let's pretend that *is* your goal. If that were the case, I'd advise you to pick an app like Tinder or Bumble because the platform is going to be a lot faster to set up and you're not going to have to spend a lot of time answering questions or thinking. All you really need are pictures, a quick bio and bam, you're on your way to Ego Boost Land.

Ok, so you've sat and considered your motives and identified your "why" for dating apps. The second question you want to ask yourself is what kind of candidate pool you're looking for. You might laugh reading the word candidate because this is a book about dating apps and you've probably never thought about that word in the same sentence as Tinder. Hear me out.

When you're on a dating app, even if it's purely to get out on dates, you become an evaluator looking at candidates, and in turn you're being evaluated as well. Just as you do when you're job hunting, you're looking for a person that's going to be a good fit, and the women on apps are wondering the same about you. Some of these "candidates" are going to be great for one date and that's it, and that's ok. You haven't stayed at each job in your life for the same amount of time have you? With that in mind, you want to ask yourself what kind of women you want to put yourself in front of.

Let's say you want an app to do the legwork on narrowing down things like religion, political affiliation, even height. In that case an app like Coffee Meets Bagel might be your match. Selecting height as the reason you don't want to match with a woman is an option on CMB. So if you're against dating women under 5"4 for some reason 1) you're welcome 2) good thing I'm not on CMB anymore.

If you want a broad dating pool, aren't sure on what parameters you have (if any), or just open to meeting all different kinds of women, then you may want to try an app like Tinder or Bumble where there's more of a mixed bag. This isn't to say there are lower quality women on either, but with 57 million users worldwide[3] there's certainly a lot of variety.

Here's something else you might want to consider: how much control do you want apps to have? Meaning, CMB and apps like it are going to control a lot more of your potential matches than Tinder will. Tinder will give you a large, mixed bag which you get to pick from, with little exclusion besides the sex of your potential matches, their desired age range and of course, the women you swipe left on. CMB will narrow down the women it shows you based on what you've told the app you don't find attractive.

This is part of making sure the app is something you want to spend time on, and not something that feels like a drag. Now I don't expect you to make decisions based on the color scheme of the app you're on–unless you have strong feelings about the color yellow in which case, stay off Bumble–but if you find the features annoying or boring, you won't enjoy it. Regardless of your objectives, your time is worth more than spending it aimlessly scrolling through an app you don't like.

The last question you want to ask yourself is, how much effort do you want to put into this? The answer might vary depending on whether you choose to do all the work yourself. You might want to start somewhere and have someone take a look and give you feedback, or just have someone create a whole profile's content for you eg. check your photos/write your bio. If you *are* doing all the work yourself though, you want to be strategic in selecting which app to download. If I were to make you a graph of how much work is required with each app, it'd look something like this:

LEAST   MOST

Tinder   Bumble   Plenty of   Coffee   Hinge   Match &
                    Fish   Meets Bagel   eHarmony

EFFORT &
TIME
REQUIRED

That's a very simplistic visual, but it's a basic breakdown of how much time/effort you need to invest to create a great profile. Thinking about how much time you want to put in will help you decide which app to download because with Tinder it'll just be a brief bio and pictures, Hinge will ask more questions and want app engagement, and apps like OkCupid or Match will ask for a lot more (and lengthier) answers to questions. Unless you want to take the time to sit down and do those, I recommend not downloading them in the first place.

Solution: Get clear on what you want!

Action Step

Grab your workbook or write it here, as long as you don't plan on lending your copy to someone. (Unless you plan on having a book club around dating apps, in which case, keep annotating here so you and the guys can discuss). Take a few minutes and answer the following questions;

- What am I looking for right now? Am I looking to use apps to find a hookup, date casually, or find a long-term partner?
- How much time do I want to spend on making my profile(s)?
- What kind of dating pool do I want?

Got it in front of you? Great. Let's talk more in depth about six apps so you can choose which one(s) will work best.

CHAPTER 2

HEY IT'S ME, KATE FROM TINDER. OR OKCUPID? OR WAS IT HINGE?

Mistake: You're on too many apps

Now you know it's necessary to be on the right app (and if you followed along, you figured out what your objectives are and you have them written down). This opens up a bunch of other questions. How do you pick? Are you supposed to be on only one? There's no definitive "right" answer to these but there are certainly ways of making those decisions.

Besides being on the *wrong* app, here's the next big mistake: being on *too many* apps. You might think being on 5 apps gives you better chances but at the end of the day, chances are it's lowering the quality of your profiles across the board. You're better off having 1-2 bomb profiles on apps you actually like instead of having 5 half-assed ones. Lowering the amount of apps you use will also force you to actually use them and be able to get a gauge on (a) whether or not you like them and (b) if they're working for you. In turn, this will prevent you from being frustrated with one and quickly moving to swipe on another.

To help you figure out where you want to be, here's a breakdown of six popular apps:

Tinder:

The biggest player in the game. Quick stat: Tinder has over 20 billion matches made every day. This is the one everyone knows, and the one with the biggest reputation (for better or for worse). Like I mentioned above, the set up for Tinder is pretty simple as you just need some pictures and a description. Using it is easy, swipe left for no, right for yes and message your matches.

Tinder **is** the best for you if you want to have a wide variety in the women you're swiping on, you want something simple and quick, and you want a quick set up that requires a lower amount of effort.

Tinder is **not** the best for you if you want to pen an elaborate description of yourself (looking at you paragraph bio holders), want to read a lot about your potential matches, and hate swiping as it feels like a game.

Bumble:

Tinder's main competitor (no shocker there as one of Tinder's co-founders made Bumble). The biggest difference between the two is that on Bumble, the women have to make the first move and matches expire. Meaning, if you match with your dream woman and she decides not to message you, the match is gone. Once a woman does send the first message, you have 24 hrs to reply, otherwise the match will disappear. Quick stat: Bumble has equal amounts of female and male users while Tinder has double the amount of men than women.[4]

Bumble **is** the best for you if you like the thought of women having to initiate, want to be on an app with an even number of women to men, and want unlimited swiping without having to pay for it.

Bumble is **not** the best for you if you hate the thought of having to wait for someone to message you, want to read a lot about your potential matches, and don't like the time crunch of 24hrs on both sides to reply.

Plenty Of Fish:

I'll be honest, it was only when I sat down to write this book that I found out POF is ranked #3 for users. The main things to know about POF are the following: you don't need to match with someone before you can message, the app offers a (skippable) personality test when you first join, and the app is a cross between dating site and matchmaking service

Plenty of Fish **is** the app for you if you want a lot of features and aren't interested in spending money to get them, don't want to be limited to only messaging the women you match with, and want to have your dating app give you a compatibility estimate.

Plenty of Fish is **not** the app for you if you want to only message women who have expressed mutual interest, don't want to learn many features, and choose exactly what information is shown on your profile.

Hinge:

Hinge branded itself as "The Relationship App" and revamped their entire interface in 2015 so it's different than the ones before. Its current slogan is "Designed to be deleted" and its features certainly reflect that. There's no swiping on this one as they wanted to move away from the game-like atmosphere of many apps. Instead, users scroll down through profiles. The app prompts you to give more information about yourself through questions and similarly to others, operates on a match system. Something unique about Hinge is that currently, the app checks in after you exchange phone numbers with a match to ask you if you went on a date and if you would like to see profiles similar to theirs. Quick stat: 75% of first dates for Hinge users turn into second dates (as of 2019.) [5]

Hinge **is** the app for you if you are seriously looking for a relationship, like the thought of not swiping, getting rid of the "game" atmosphere, and want a more involved app.

Hinge is **not** the app for you if you want the ego boost of seeing a bunch of matches, want to use dating apps for casual dating and are sure you don't want a relationship, and don't want to pay for extended features such as seeing everyone who liked you.

Coffee Meets Bagel:

CMB is definitely a "less is more" kind of app. Here you don't go through multiple profiles; you're shown a limited amount of people each day who you can say yes or no to. In this app, you're encouraged to comment on profiles before you match. Quick stat: in beta testing, CMB found those who commented on their potential matches had a 25% increase in those who liked them back[6]. Another big difference: when you say no to someone, you can tell the app exactly why. Meaning, if you don't want to talk to a woman because she's too tall, you can mark it. Over time, the app learns what you do/don't like.

CMB **is** the app for you if you think of height, ethnicity, religion, etc as dealbreakers, want to train an algorithm on your preferences, and would rather look at one profile at a time.

CMB is **not** the app for you if you want the broadest dating pool, would rather not provide a bunch of info to potential matches, want to see several profiles at a time instead of just one, and are looking to *only* casually date.

OkCupid:

OKC is more long-form, and will ask you a lot of questions both about yourself and your preferences when you're building a profile in order to put their very complex algorithm to work. The questions range from religion, to political affiliation, to media preferences, to lifestyle questions. The app also features much more specificity when it comes to setting up your profile. It includes options for 13 different sexual orientations as well as 22 gender options which allows users to either narrow or broaden their potential matches based on preferences[7]. Unlike POF, OkC does use a match system so you're not free to message at random, you have to match with a person first.[8] Quick stat: The average age for OKC users is 24-35.

OKC **is** the app for you if you want to read longer bios than the quick fix found on Tinder, want a more complex algorithm at work, and want to dedicate time on the app to tell potential dates a lot about yourself.

OKC is **not** the app for you if you don't want to be on a very politically liberal, diversity-focused platform, don't have the time/energy for writing a bunch about yourself or answering questions, and want to swipe on profiles.

Match/eHarmony:

Putting these two together here as a final note. If you want to spend the money on a dating service that's available as an app, these two are the biggest ones. Quick stat: They've been around longer than all the other apps and boast an impressive amount of users. Prices range from $36 for a month on Match to $50 for a month long membership on eHarmony. Know that the profiles here are lengthier, so expect to spend more time than on other apps, especially on the set-up.

Match/eHarmony **are** the app(s) for you if you like the thought of an established dating pool, are seriously looking for a relationship, and want to test out a lot of features.

Match/eHarmony are **not** the app(s) for you if you want to try out online dating without paying for a subscription, want a quick set up process, and don't want to spend a lot of time building a profile.

The solution: get on the right app (s) and delete the rest!

Action Step

Compare your list of objectives from your workbook with the apps on your phone (or the list I've provided here). Every man's phone will be different but I recommend not being on more than 2 apps, 3 max. By now you should have a general idea of which one(s) will be the best for you. Pick accordingly and I'll see you in the next chapter.

PART II

YOUR PROFILE

CHAPTER 3

ARE YOU TAKING PICTURES WITH YOUR 2012 IPOD TOUCH?

The Mistake: Your pictures suck (or just don't shine!)

Welcome to actually creating (or re-creating) your profile. Now that you've picked your app(s) let's talk about your photos. You bought a book and made it this far so I'm confident in assuming you're willing to put some effort into this. Yes? Hopefully you're nodding your head in agreement, but even if not, chances are you need to hear this.

If we were together in person, I'd have you repeat the following after me: I promise to start taking my photos seriously. Since we're not in person, I'll just strongly recommend you underline and say it out loud to yourself, at least 5 times. I might seem like I'm being overly insistent but listen, your pictures are the FIRST thing a woman will look at when she sees your profile. Sounds like a no brainer to have good ones, right? The problem is most men would agree with that statement and yet, there's so many profiles out there with pictures from 2010 featuring poorly cropped-out ex girlfriends and a college haircut. We get it, the "effortless" mussed waves wooed the ladies back then, but we're no longer in a poorly lit basement.

I'm not exaggerating when I say I've watched groups of women gathered around a phone, cringing as they look through a guy's photos. So in no particular order, here's a list of things I've heard women complain about when it comes to men's dating profile pictures:

1. In every picture, you're wearing sunglasses.

    So you love those Ray-Bans or maybe the outdoors is your favorite place to be. Good for you, however, if someone's going to decide you're attractive and they want to talk to you, it's super helpful when they can see your face. If one of your pictures is on the beach and you're wearing shades, that's fine. Just don't make a woman spend minutes wondering what's hiding underneath. It may seem like a great strategy to look cooler, or hide any insecurities, but it raises more questions than matches. If you have no other photos except you on vacation, women will wonder if you're a person with a real job who never takes photos or a douche who wants to show off their money.

2. Every picture is a selfie taken from slightly different angles.

    Maybe being photographed isn't your jam. That's fine, but if the goal of pictures is to communicate something, not much is being communicated by 5 selfies. 1 is fine but after 3 your profile screams that you're either vain or boring even if you're not actually either. If you don't know where to get pictures of yourself, try checking the pictures you're tagged in on social media. Chances are you have some group ones. Alternatively, you can also look through pictures from work events. For pictures of just you, next time you're at an event or out with friends, just ask someone and pass them your phone. Or use your latest work headshot. Or ask a stranger on the street to grab one of you and a burrito if you can't fathom asking a friend.

3. Every picture on your profile is a group picture.

    No woman wants to play *Where's Waldo?* when they're looking at your profile. Here's what happens: the woman tries to find the person who appears most often and is therefore most likely to be the profile owner. She then hopes he's the attractive one. Most of the time she'll get frustrated and if it's too hard, your profile will be promptly rejected. You want a woman to be excited to talk to you, not hoping "Charlie" is the blond one in the back. Group pictures can be great for showing your hobbies and groups of friends but make sure the women looking at your profile actually know what **you** look like. On that note, *please* don't take this as a reason to crop group photos to just show you. Unless you're a Photoshop whiz, you'll end up with a pixelated mess full of other people's elbows.

4. Your pictures are vastly different than reality.

    The first time I ever went on a date with a guy I met on Tinder, I was debating what he'd look like in person. The cause for my dilemma? His second and third pictures looked pretty different (by that I mean they looked like sibling photos) and I couldn't tell which one was more recent. Imagine my face when I looked down the aisle of the Barnes and Noble we were meeting at and saw neither. After a very awkward "um,?" I got over the initial shock and our coffee date ended up fine but I always wondered how old his pictures have to be if none of them resembled him.

    Even if you're upfront about not resembling your pictures much, it's still a shock (which I'm sure you've experienced if you've ever gone on a date with a woman who didn't match her pictures). A year after that first encounter in B&N, during another first date, the first thing he said when he got in my car was "Hey! I know I look nothing like my picture, sorry!" In this case, it was because his haircut was totally different than in his profile. Again, the date itself went fine but if you can avoid confusing women, do so. Now I'm not saying you have to take a picture immediately after every haircut but if you shave off the beard pictured across your whole profile, you'll shock someone when you meet up. Or she'll hang up a FaceTime saying, "Sorry, dialed the wrong number!".

5. You have a picture with a woman obviously cropped out or her face blacked out.

It baffles me that men will use a picture like this and expect to get away with it. In case there's any doubt, let me assure you that these pictures do **not** impress. Using one of these pictures gives off the impression that so few pictures of you exist you had to resort to one with an ex, which can be a dealbreaker for some women. Additionally, blacking out a woman's face screams petty. Know that any picture of just you and a woman in it will draw the "Is that his ex-girlfriend or his sister?" question. Do not take this to mean you can't use a group picture featuring women, just be conscious of using ones where you are pictured alone with one woman.

Those are some general don'ts. However, if you only take one thing away from this chapter let it be this: picture resolution matters!

People want to date high-quality people.

You're a high-quality guy so why do your pictures look like you took them on a Razor a decade ago? The closer you can get to HD the better and honestly, an HD shot of a man wearing sunglasses in 5 group pictures is preferable to a lot of other profiles out there. This doesn't mean you need to hire a photographer and do a shoot. An iPhone will do just fine, and if you have a newer one and can use portrait mode, all the better. If you do have photoshoot pictures, feel free to use them, as long as you don't put up five pictures from the same shoot. See my point above regarding selfies.

Statistically speaking, there's a few things which will increase the likelihood of women swiping right on your profile. Things like, looking away from the camera in your first picture, or having an animal in your photos[9] (that does not include holding a bass you just caught—please skip the fish!).

To summarize, here are the general guidelines you want to follow when picking out your pictures:

- High resolution is always better so the higher the photo quality, the better your profile will look as a whole. HD is best but this can easily come from an iPhone/Android; you don't need a fancy camera.

- Your first picture should look very accurate to what you look like right now, so if you recently shaved your beard make sure your first picture is clean shaven.
- Your first picture should feature just a clear picture of you and should be free of sunglasses/other obstructions.
- You should include a mix of pictures of you alone and with a group.

Last thing to note: a profile should tell the women about you, and pictures can be a huge tool to showcase hobbies/interests. Love hiking? Use a picture of yourself at one of your favorite spots. Love Marvel? Use that picture of your group of friends at the last premiere. You get my point, so just choose your photos and then ask, "What does a woman looking at my profile learn?"

Story time: I once had a client who was uber successful in his field ask why his profile wasn't getting any traction. When I looked through his photos, I realized almost all of them had a private jet. Either he was sitting in one, or he was pictured on the stairs of it, or it was behind him… you get the idea. This quickly set off red flags for me, although on the surface it might seem like a good thing. Private jets = good with money = good for a relationship, right?

Some women might get super excited about that but here's the thing: when a woman looks at a profile, in about 5 seconds she comes to a conclusion about the man she's viewing. (And it may be less than that, as research indicates people can form first impressions as quickly as within 1/10 of a second)[10]. It could be a good one, it could be a bad one, it could also be indifferent but either way, within a few seconds, she's made it.

The problem with the 5 private jet photos is that if I'm the woman viewing this profile, when those first few seconds are up, what am I basing my conclusion off of? Just the jets. So if I like the thought of flying on a private jet, I'll think you're great. If I don't because it tells me nothing about your personality, then I won't. More important than whether I like the fact that you're on private jets often, is that this is the only thing I've learned about you.

Yes, you've worked hard and now you get to ride in private jets. That's commendable but it shouldn't be the *only* thing I learn about you looking through your profile. If it's a big part of your life or just something cool you want to showcase, absolutely throw a picture in there. Just don't make it the only one.

A way to make picture selection easier is to imagine you're giving a woman your elevator pitch. You have six photos so what six things do you want to tell her? Remember that you're building a dating profile not a Facebook profile so you have limited real estate (especially on apps like Tinder/Bumble). Make it count.

Action Step
Take a look at your profile considering the common mistakes I mentioned. Get rid of excessive selfies, group shots, and photos of you that don't look like you. Most importantly, get rid of anything that isn't in HD. Pro tip: make an album of high-res photos on your phone, ideally with a variety of locations. Make sure most are of you alone. Go through and select 5 to upload. Don't have 5? Now you have your homework for the next week. Do *not* continue until you have great photos up.

CHAPTER 4

OH, SO YOU LIKE SPORTS AND HIKING? NEVER HEARD THAT ONE BEFORE.

The Mistake: Your Bio Needs Work

✱Note: The bio info I have here is pretty specific to short bio apps like Tinder and Bumble. If you're planning on using apps like OkCupid, the gist of it will still be relevant, but you'll want to plan to write more than I instruct here.

Now that we've covered pictures, let's move on to your bio. If you're working on a profile on OkC or Hinge, it will be a part of several other components. Regardless of which app you use, it's still important to know how to write an engaging, effective bio.

Let me first clear something up, it's not often that I see profiles with bad bios. The key mistake men make when it comes to their bio is assuming that it doesn't matter. You might think the only important part of your profile are the pictures, and I'm here to set you straight.

Let me walk you through the thought process that happened inside my brain every day I was swiping through dating apps:

- I'd see a man I thought was attractive and open his profile to read more about him
- His bio would be either blank, consist of three words, or terrible.
- I'd swipe left or keep scrolling.

I used to have a rule that if a man didn't have a bio, it was an automatic no. Not every woman is going to do the same—there will be some who decide solely based on your pictures—but that shouldn't keep you from having a bio. Sure, you could just crush the picture aspect and have a solid 6 out of 10 profile but you bought this book to be great and not settle for good.

Your bio serves three basic functions:

1) It shows you give a damn.
2) Gives more information about you but just as or even *more* important is its third purpose ↓
3) It helps women make the first move.

The first and second might *seem* self-explanatory but I'm going to elaborate on them anyway. Using Tinder as an example, 62% of users worldwide are men[11]. Meaning, your profile is one fish in a very big sea. Since many of those 6.2 million men don't have a bio, by leaving yours empty you are joining the majority. Having a blank description communicates you couldn't even be bothered to write a few lines, which is not a great first impression on the women you're trying to date. Your bio is the first step to standing out and helping women get to know who you are, not just what you look like.

More on the third function of a bio in a second, but first, let's take a look at some of the most common mistakes made with bios.

1) Reiterating your age. If it's an app like Tinder or Bumble, they can see that right off the bat, so why are you repeating yourself? (Unless for some reason there's an error in the age your profile is displaying).

2) Words like "adventure". In case you missed the chapter title, here's another reminder to leave used and cliched phrases behind.

3) Saying you love The Office.

Also, here's a short list of phrases to avoid (or delete):

- "Not here just for hookups"
- "Looking for a relationship or just friends"
- Emoji only bios
- Emojis in general (that's just my opinion)
- "SWIPE LEFT IF YOU" (aggressive and unnecessary, unless there is an absolute legitimate dealbreaker)

Here's that third reason why a bio is important. Remember how I said it helps a woman make the first move? Imagine you're at a bar and you see a beautiful woman holding a sign that says "Ask me about traveling to Chile." How easy would it be to walk up, introduce yourself, and then ask about Chile?

If you write a good bio, you're able to give women a quick look into your personality and then provide a roadmap for them to engage with you. Instead of wondering what to say, women are now confidently sending you messages. Having a strong bio will help you stand out from the other 6.2 million profiles a woman is swiping through. A lot of people swipe through their dating apps distracted or while they're watching TV, so if you want to catch a woman's eye there has to be something different going on in your profile. Like I said at the start of chapter, will every woman read every bio? No. Will some women just base their swiping decisions on pictures alone? Absolutely. Neither of those things should preclude you from having a strong bio to interest the women that **do** read it.

This also helps when you send the first message. More on how to deliver something first later, but for now consider this: when you send a first message, the woman who receives it will then look at your profile and decide if she's going to reply. If your profile looks just like every other guy's, the chances of her responding positively or even responding at all go down. Think of it like you'd consider networking for your dream job. If your photos are your elevator pitch, your bio is your ask. Would you want to be in the stack sitting on some corporate recruiter's desk email inbox? No, you'd want your resume to be the one they glance at and call into an interview immediately.

So what makes a strong bio? When I sat down to write this handbook, I asked myself, "From the hundreds of bios I've seen and all the ones I've edited, what do the strongest share?" I boiled it down to the following:

Super Swipeable Bios

- Descriptive → teaches at least 3 things
- Short → not an enormous paragraph.
- Have a CTA (call to action) → encourage a woman to respond.

That's it. If you already have a dating profile, check it right now and check for those three things specifically.

1) If I were to look at it for the first time, would I learn 3 things about you that I don't already know from the rest of your profile?
2) How's the length of your bio? Hint: If it's less than a sentence, it's too short. You have some flexibility here but I'd say on an app like Tinder, keep it between three and six sentences max.
3) Is there a CTA? Meaning, am I encouraged to ask you a question, answer a question, make a guess etc?

When I'm editing a profile, the difference between a good one and a great one is that the good ones always leave a woman hanging. The CTA is a key part to the bio and will improve the number of matches you have, the number of women who message you first, and the number of women who respond to your messages.

So what should your CTA be? I'd say it depends on your personality but here are two ideas:

- Play "Two truths and a lie".
- Say "Guess the last place I traveled/favorite city/favorite food etc and dinner's on me"

A large portion of the profile rewrites I do end in some variation of guessing a correct answer or giving the "best" idea and "winning" dinner or coffee etc. This has a ton of potential, as it won't just be fun but might also provide you new restaurants and/or experiences. Not to mention a date to check them out with. Win-win.

Story time: I once had a client read the bio I wrote for him and told me he felt like he'd be buying a lot of dinners and didn't want to advertise that. To that point, I'll tell you the same thing I told him, it's not about the dinner. If you want to say coffee and not "overcommit" yourself, feel free. At the end of the day, the purpose of a CTA is to motivate someone to message you.

(PS. Just for the record, I've never had a client come back broke from purchasing too many dinners for women.)

Action Step
Either edit your bio with the 3 criteria I mentioned above, or use the checklist included in your workbook to guide you while you write. Can't think of what to write? Imagine you have an elevator ride to describe yourself, write down what comes to mind first. Or, ask a friend how they'd describe you in only 3 sentences. Have fun here, play around with what you talk about and/ or the format. Double check that you included a CTA.

CHAPTER 5

HELLO, KYLE? ARE YOU THERE?

The Mistake: You Don't Use App Features or Ever Update Anything

I remember when I used to go on dating apps that featured icebreaker questions and see a bunch of blank spaces. I rolled my eyes many times wondering how lazy men had to be to not answer what their favorite food was. Like I said before, better to have a great, short Tinder profile than a crappy Hinge profile.

Note: This next part I'm about to cover is most relevant if you're using apps like Hinge or Coffee Meets Bagel but for my Tinder users out there, it's still important for you to know.

One of the biggest mistakes men make when downloading a dating app is ignoring the features available. For example, on Tinder, there's music integration where you can include a song from Spotify. Is the lack of an "anthem" going to make or break your profile? No. Could having an anthem give it a boost? Absolutely.

Additional features are what take a profile from an 8/9 to 10. The reason for this is that just like having a bio gives a woman an easy in to talk to you, so do the extra features, like your Spotify song. If you happen to list her current favorite song, or if she likes the artist, or even **hates** the artist, you've now provided something easy for her to engage with.

For apps like Hinge, many have extra questions you can answer eg. OkC shuffles. If you don't fill them out, it looks like you don't care. Most women don't want to talk to or go out with a man who's too cool to answer some questions or add a song. Not to say some women might not care, but like the rest of the book, better to have it and make your profile that much better than the opposite scenario.

The fact is, being active on an app is going to increase your shot. If you don't open your Tinder for three weeks, and a woman can see that, why would she send you a message? If you've been inactive for a month, a woman's desire to even *try* to talk to you will lessen.

Being inactive and leaving your profile for months at a time communicates you either don't care or don't check it, neither of which will motivate a woman to talk to you. It's like leaving a placard at a bar that says "John used to hang out here, but he hasn't been back in a while." No one is going to wait for you to come back to the bar, and no woman will sit by her phone as she anxiously awaits your online return. Out of sight out of mind applies here, so know that if a woman sends you a message and you reply 2 weeks later, her enthusiasm for you has dropped significantly.

I'm not telling you to open Tinder 8x a day so that you appear active on it. You don't have time for that and your time is valuable. Checking whatever app you're on at least once every few days, however, will make sure you're seeing new matches, messages, and your profile looks like it belongs to someone who will actively respond.

If you do things like answer all of the questions on your profile, not only will it give someone more information about you, but it will set you apart from the guy who has a blank bio and has "Lol" as the answer to what his favorite movie is.

I'll leave you with this: If you have something, use it, otherwise what's the point of having it? In the case of dating apps, if you're going to use it, wield all the features possible and use it to maximize benefits for yourself. Chances are that adding your favorite song or answering questions for five minutes is going to be the easiest thing on your To Do list today.

Action Step

Now that you have your app, check its features. Google it if you have no idea. On Tinder? Upload what you're listening to on Spotify. Using OkC? Answer some questions. This is a great point to double and triple check that you're only keeping the apps that you actually like to use. If you're *really* bored using a feature, delete the app. Make it a plan that whatever you decide to use, you'll log on at least 3 times this week.

PART III

CHAPTER 6

HEY IT'S ME, THAT WOMAN WHO YOU'RE NOT INTERESTED IN. WANNA CHAT?

The Mistake: You're swiping right on everyone.

I used to have a roommate, let's call him Chris, who *really* liked being on Tinder. Sometimes when we'd all be sitting in his room, I'd watch him swipe. I always found it shocking he barely looked at the women before swiping (almost always right) and could barely keep up with how fast he was going. Pretty often, he'd tell me he was out of right swipes and had to wait to try more later.

I had no idea what that meant, but after more research, soon had my answer.

Tinder, it turns out, limits the amount of likes you can give out. If you run out, you have to wait 12 hours until the counter resets unless you pay for more swipes which Chris wasn't interested in doing. Many men I've met since are.

Back then, I was shocked that Chris was hitting some sort of limit and honestly chalked it up to Chris being Chris. That is, until I started hearing it from multiple guys who told me about having to wait because they'd used up all their likes for the day. This blew my mind because when I looked it up, Tinder allowed 100 likes per 12 hours (current estimates say it's between 50-100 now and depends on your profile). This meant these guys were trying to swipe right on *more than 200 women a day*.

The most interesting part to me was their reactions to the question "Why?". I never really got an answer besides some variation of "It'll give me the best shot".

That's some hot BS. Actually, "over-swiping" lessens your number of matches as the algorithm will start showing your profile to fewer people[12].

Also, randomly matching might increase the quantity of matches you get but it'll certainly decrease the quality. This is the reason why some apps actually refuse to show you more than a few or even one profile at a time (Coffee Meets Bagel for example). So if you're currently swiping right on everyone, stop.

I fully believe a large part of the reason people complain about their Tinder matches is because they're a) not excited to talk to them because none of them stand out or b) their matches list is full of people they'd never want to go out with. I don't think this means you should be so selective you don't match with anyone, but I do think you should pay attention or at least read a bit instead of casting the widest possible net.

Like I said in the first chapter, if you want a lot of variety in the dating pool, pick an app that gives you that freedom of choice, without the swiping. Not only will you avoid feeling like you're running out of likes but it'll also make you more excited to see messages now that you've taken out all the women you barely glanced at to begin with.

In today's world of picturesque social media feeds and FOMO, it can seem like you *should* match with as many women. It's okay to be selective because it will make your dating app experience smoother and more enjoyable.

Balance is key here. Don't take that to mean you should only swipe right on the woman you think could be your soulmate.

An important note here is that some people swipe right on everyone not to truly get the best shot possible, but instead, to get as many matches as possible. Here's the thing though: **no one cares.** Having a bunch of matches means nothing if that's all they are.

Unless you're switching careers and you've found a job where you're paid to do nothing except accrue as many matches as possible, leave that attitude at the door. (If you have, please email me immediately, this book stuff is hard work.) There are better ways to create or improve your self image that don't comprise of feeling validated through droves of women deeming you attractive enough to slide their thumb to the right on a dating app.

For reference, guess how many women have ever told me they're out of swipes? Zero. Consider that with a higher percentage of Tinder users being men, women actually have more options. They're not running out, so stop acting like the world will end if you don't have enough matches and use matching for what it is: mutual interest.

Action Step
In your workbook, sign the commitment. This week, only swipe/match with women you'd actually take on a date. Read their bios and only swipe on women who you'd be stoked to take to dinner on Friday. If you're a serial run-out-of-swipes guy, see how long you can go before encountering that error message. Consider why you want to match with someone, and don't just have "She's hot." as the answer.

CHAPTER 7

"WHAT'S UP?"
I'M BORED, THAT'S WHAT'S UP.

The Mistake: Your first message is the same as every other guy.

If I had $1 for every time a guy on Tinder sent the word, "Hey." as his first message, I'd be set for life. I probably wouldn't be writing this book, that's how much money I'd have. (Kidding, I'd still write it to stop hearing women complain.)

I get it, you're not sure what to say to open a conversation so "Hey" seems like the safest bet. That might be true, but saying "Hey", is the equivalent of saying a casual "Hey." as you pass someone on the street and keep walking without looking back. If a woman came up to you and only said "Hey.", would you be amped to talk to her? You might respond but it's not going to be the smoothest conversation it could be.

Don't use the same message everyone else does. Women get so many "Hey" messages that oftentimes, they ignore them off the bat. We know it doesn't take effort to hit three keys. We know you don't know the perfect opener, but you have to come up with something better than "Hey." if you want a shot at catching anyone's attention.

Some women might respond to that "Hey." but I've never met a woman who was excited or intrigued when she received one. Would you rather have someone half-heartedly reply or think to herself "Wow, that was good. I'm going to reply right away" when she sees your message? Standing out in your first message is the equivalent of seeing a Facebook ad and thinking "Damn, they got me with this one" and deciding to buy without a single hesitation because you know you *need* it.

Other first messages to avoid:

- Hey what's up?
- Hey beautiful/gorgeous/sexy/baby/etc.
- A pun about her name (unless it's the best one of all time, I bet you she gets them daily)

Let me show you how to shine in this area of dating apps. It all starts with paying attention. If you think back to the reasons why having a strong bio is important, the same thing can be said for hers. If she has a strong bio, that helps you out a lot, as it tells you what you can comment on.

Even if she doesn't, there's still things you can look for which will help you craft the first message.

1) Depending on the app, you might be able to see mutual friends.
2) If you're on Coffee Meets Bagel, you can tell her she's the best bagel you've had in awhile. Cheesy? Yes. Effective though.
3) If you're on Tinder and you see their Spotify song, comment on that! Use it as a tool to either tease them about it, agree with them and geek out, or ask them who the artist is and why they chose it.

Other things to try:
- Comment on a mutual interest
- Comment on a mutual disinterest
- Tell her you bet she can't solve the two truths and a lie in your bio.
- Tell her there's free dinner instructions in your bio if you have a guessing CTA.
- Tell her she looks like the kind of woman who'd like to go to a bookstore (insert: concert, other location, etc)
- If you're funny, make a joke. If you're not, don't.

The key to executing a great first message is to pay attention: take the time and energy to go read her bio, look through her pictures, and show you put some effort in.

A first message might be as simple as taking a wild shot at guessing their location from one of their pictures. If you see a woman standing on a hill, you could very well message her and say "I bet you're at _____ in your third picture". If she responds and says you're wrong, how easy it is to say "Guess I lost, owe you dinner then".

I've said it before and I'll say it again: it doesn't take much, just put some effort in.

Keep in mind that some women will send you a first message, but others won't. That being said, having a strong bio will make getting a response to your initial message much more likely as she will probably check your profile when she reads it. I once had a match correctly guess my job because of the corner of a poster he saw in the background of one of my pictures and I was so impressed I messaged him back immediately with the sole purpose of asking *him* out.

Also, know that sending a good first message puts you closer to the bottom of a woman's dating app funnel.

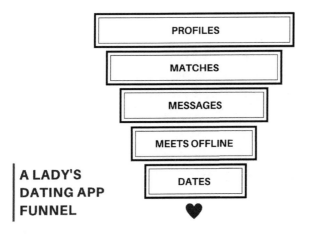

A LADY'S DATING APP FUNNEL

Sending a message is important because it'll differentiate you from the bunch of silent matches women get (which are plenty). Especially if a woman catches your eye, take a minute and read through her profile before you send her a message.

Action Step
Head to your workbook and answer the questions included. From now on, challenge yourself to start a conversation with something that is not "Hey." or a pun about her name. Read through the bios from the next 5 women who you want to talk to and send them each a different message. Imagine what you'd say if they were standing in front of you and go from there, don't overthink it. The goal isn't to send the "perfect" first message, it's just to be genuine and stand out from the many others she's received today.

CHAPTER 8

SO, IT'S BEEN 6 MONTHS. ARE WE EVER GOING TO GO OUT?

The Mistake: You're not moving offline.

One more chapter and you're golden, so let's get to it. Here's your chance to implement everything I've previously stated in the other chapters and get way ahead of the game. Anyone can tell you to pick better photos or write a better bio (and that's what most sellers online will help you with) but here's my best tip of all time. It all boils down to:

Women don't want pen pals.

Underline it, circle it, text it to a friend, get it in your head. *Women do not want pen pals.* We are in the 21st century, the days of penning your life story by candlelight are far gone. Too often, the biggest mistake I watch men make is staying on apps for longer than necessary. They text back and forth on the app incessantly or they move off the app to text from their phones but leave it there. If your goal in life is to emulate that slightly disturbing relationship from the movie *Her*, then congratulations. In both scenarios a man is in a relationship with a personality on a piece of technology and I'm willing to bet you don't want that. You might not want a relationship right now but chances are, your idea of success on dating apps includes you know, dating.

If that's the case, you need to be intentional in using dating apps as *a tool and method of introduction to meeting women*. If you follow what I've outlined, your profile will be high level, but make sure you don't get caught up in that and lose sight of what matters. Otherwise, you'll just fall into the category of random guy from Tinder/Hinge/Bumble who she talked to two years ago. Or you could end up as the contact in her phone that she doesn't recognize.

Having a high level profile and not moving offline is the same thing as meeting a woman somewhere, exchanging numbers and then having a random contact in your phone you won't remember in 2 weeks. Keyword: forgettable.

Don't want to be that guy? Then avoid having a three week conversation solely based over the messaging on Tinder or iMessage (or whatever non-iPhone users use, you heathens). You have to make the effort to move off the screen and move into real life.

Suggesting a date might seem challenging but just like everything else, you just have to do it. Worst case scenario she doesn't respond and that's that. Best case scenario you're actually able to go on dates. Maybe you're internally scoffing thinking "Psh, asking women on dates is a breeze, I just don't want to." Ok good for you Casanova, but humor me will you?

Should you take this to mean you should ask out every single match? No, not necessarily. That being said, if you start swiping with the mentality of matching with women you might want to go on a date with, then asking some will be much easier.

Also, you could start texting someone and realize there's no way you want to see them. That's fine. Tell them you don't think you connect and wish them a great day. Instead of ghosting a woman because you think that's nicer or because it's easier, it's not, so let her know.

It *should* be common courtesy and trust me, I tell women this same thing since it seems to be a problem for everyone. Being utterly swipeable doesn't just mean attracting great women to your profile, it also means being respectful in your interactions. If you're a high performer or just consider yourself a great guy in general but use silence across apps and texts to convey your lack of interest, I would reconsider that.

Respect should go without saying but from the women I talked to while writing, it isn't. Let's make something crystal clear, a woman on a dating app is not just a target for sexual innuendo and disrespect. On the other end of an interaction is a person who deserves respect, and a woman who agrees to meet with you for a date is doing that, agreeing to a date. Not agreeing to having sex with you.

When I surveyed women on what they would tell men if they could impart one piece of advice, almost every single one said the same thing: "Be honest about your intentions from the get go". If you're looking for just sex, I would say so on your profile. It would save you time and match you with women who are also looking for that. Ghosting someone because **you** didn't disclose what **you** were really looking for and then **you** realized **you** weren't going to get it, is just plain childish.

Ok, I'll get off my soap box.

Asking a woman out will also be key in differentiating yourself from the other men out there. I can't tell you how many times I've heard a woman talk about the lack of movement with a man after exchanging numbers with a match or messaging back and forth for a week. A lot of the time, women want to go out with a man and are waiting in awkward limbo hoping he'll ask her out.

Remember that some women will feel comfortable asking you out, just as some will send the first message, but not all will. So if you're interested in meeting her face to face, ask her.

I know you might use Passport or other premium features that allow you to match with people outside your immediate area. In those cases, you might be talking to someone you can't physically meet with for a while. If that's the case, then use the technology at your disposal and call them on Facetime. If not, you'll risk her wondering if she's going to end up catfished, and on your end, you won't be able to gauge whether or not you want to keep talking to her. There isn't a set amount of time you have to wait before you ask her to coffee/dinner/brunch/concerts/etc. so whenever you feel that yes this is a woman you want to meet, do it.

Action Step:
Grab your workbook and your phone and answer the following questions:

1) If you know or notice you don't ask many of your matches out, ask yourself why? Are you not interested in them? Scared of being rejected? Feel like it's too much work?
2) Go through your recent conversations on the app you're using and honestly ask yourself, who you would want to meet in person. If you've been texting a woman more than 3 days, it's probably a sign that it's time to move offline.
3) Reaffirm what you're looking for. Do you want to just date a few women casually? Do you want to find a relationship? Whatever it is, if you haven't discussed it already, do it now.

« CONCLUSION »

You've made it to the end, sending you a virtual high five. If you've been following along with the action steps, you might already be done revamping but just in case you weren't, let's recap.

Here's the 8-step process for dating app success:

1) Choose the right app(s) for what you want
2) Get off the unnecessary apps (or the ones you hate)
3) Use quality photos
4) Have a kickass bio
5) Use features & stay active
6) Swipe selectively
7) Send a solid first message
8) Get off the app and in person

And remember: be clear about your intentions.

That's it. It's my hope that after reading this handbook, you can avoid the frustration and lack of results that so many men have. You have the information now to make changes and move towards being utterly swipeable. With this info you can tap and swipe with confidence and flood the dating app world with kick ass profiles and activity. Gone are the days of wondering "Wtf do women want?" because you my friend, now have the answer.

Like anything in life though, this process only works if you do ALL of the steps. Don't just pick an app and update photos, you *might* get better results doing that but you're here to be high-level, so get out there and do it **well**. Chances are, you can knock out steps 1 &2 today and be at least 25% of the way there. It only takes 10 seconds to download or delete a dating app after all. After that, your work is cut out for you.

Your new era of dating awaits, so grab your phone and happy swiping!

NOTES

1. Kopf, Dan. "Around 40% of American Couples Now First Meet Online." Quartz. QZ, February 12, 2019.
2. Cacioppo, J. T., Cacioppo, S., Gonzaga, G. C., Ogburn, E. L., & VanderWeele, T. J. (2013). Marital satisfaction and break-ups differ across on-line and off-line meeting venues. Proceedings of the National Academy of Sciences, 110(25), 10135-10140.
3. Iqbal, Mansoor. "Tinder Revenue and Usage Statistics (2018)." Business of Apps, February 27, 2019.
4. Photofeeler. "Bumble Vs. Tinder: Which One Is BETTER for Guys? For Women?" Profiled, March 24, 2019.
5. "Hinge Information, Statistics, Facts and History." Dating Sites Reviews. eSilverStrike Consulting Inc., n.d.
6. Perez, Sarah. "Coffee Meets Bagel Goes Anti-Tinder with a Redesign Focused on Profiles, Conversations." TechCrunch. TechCrunch, December 11, 2018.
7. OkCupid. "Non Binary Profile Options." OkCupid Help, December 3, 2019.
8. Stodart, Leah. "OkCupid Review 2019: A Hip Dating Site That's Way Less Lame than the Competition." Mashable, September 4, 2019.
9. Klinenberg, E., & Ansari, A. (2015). *Modern Romance*. New York: The Penguin Press.

10. Wargo, Eric. "How Many Seconds to a First Impression?" Association for Psychological Science–APS. Association for Psychological Science, July 2006.

11. Iqbal, Mansoor. "Tinder Revenue and Usage Statistics (2018)." Business of Apps, February 27, 2019.

12. Tiffany, Kaitlyn. "How the Tinder Algorithm Actually Works." Vox. Vox Media, March 18, 2019.

ACKNOWLEDGEMENTS

First of all, a big thank you goes to you, reader. Thanks for coming along on this journey and making my dream of authorship possible. To my sister Andrea who kickstarted this whole thing, thanks for making that bet. Your support over the course of my life has been invaluable, thanks for always reminding me to laugh. To the OG Nicole, thanks for trusting me to write your profile; who knew we'd end up here? Thanks for being the first to dub me the #TinderGod and restoring my faith in myself when I needed it.

Kevin Curry, you were the first professor to encourage my "crazy" idea. Thank you for all the articles over the years, the ideas, and the accountability you provided. You nurtured this passion in me and without you, none of this would have happened. To my roommates, Jade and Shelby, thank you for enduring the incessant conversations about dating apps and encouraging me to keep going. Shelby, without you my thesis would never have happened and neither would this book. Marcus Johnson, thanks for helping me see I'm more than just one thing and that anything's possible.

To my boss, Dave, without your support I would have thought this project was too far fetched to pursue. Thanks for never stifling my creative ambitions and pouring love into me over the years. To my parents, thanks for politely nodding along while I talked about my book and never judging how much I like to talk about online dating. You helped me always dream bigger. To Lily and Alecia, thanks for telling me to stop procrastinating out of fear and to just do it! I see more opportunity in the world thanks to you. To my coach Olivia, one of my life's greatest blessings was connecting with you. You have helped me find so much joy and ease in life. This is only the beginning and I can't wait to see what's in front of us to celebrate.

To my folks at SPS, I *literally* couldn't have done this without you. Chandler, thanks for helping me believe this was possible and telling me I should share my ideas. Dillon, you're one of the most genuine people I've ever met; thank you for telling me this was viable and helping me see the vision of how to bring it to life. Gary, thanks for never giving up on me and answering every question I had. Lisa and Matt, you pushed a stranger to follow through, thanks friends! To my editor, Haylee, bless you for taking on my rambles and helping me do better. Thank goodness for our random pairing.

To all my clients, thank you for your business and trust. To all the women who've given me feedback and opinions over the years, your opinions have been invaluable in shaping my work. Special shoutout to Mariah, Rosi, Rachel*, Melanie, and Lily for their direct feedback with this handbook. To my best friend Danika, there are no words to describe how grateful I am to have your friendship but I'll try. Thank you for the countless brainstorming, editing, and discussion; life is so much brighter because you're in it.

Lastly, to my fiancé, Dominic: thank the Lord that (1) Tinder exists and (2) Blanca swiped right on you for me so I didn't swipe no for a 7th time because of your profile's many selfies. Thank you for lovingly calling me out, giving me unconditional support, and joining me in this crazy journey of life. Love you long time.

ABOUT CAMILA ARGUELLO

Originally from Bogotá, Colombia, Camila Arguello has since lived in five different cities in the US. She discovered her passion for dating apps while navigating the highs and lows of online dating. A graduate of Linfield College (now University), she holds a B.A. in International Relations and a B.S. in Psychology, with a focus on the intersection of romance, tech, and politics. When she's not editing profiles or talking about the modern era of romance, she enjoys food tours, dystopian fiction, and drinking mojitos with her best friend. Today, she is a retired Tinder-ee and lives in the Bay Area with her fiancé Dominic and their cat Rex Gladium.

Lets keep this party going

If you can't already tell, I love talking about dating. I truly believe transparency and communication are the keys to changing the way we date. That in mind, I'd love to talk further about it and share any resources I can. Maybe you know something I don't and we could have a great conversation about it. So if you have questions or just want to chat about how much better swiping is for you now (that's always the goal!), connect with me on social. You can find me here on Instagram: @camila_arri! If you hate IG, send me an email at camila@swipeablebook.com. Talk soon!

Quick favor

Here's the thing, dating changes on a mass scale only if we work together. If you learned anything from *Swipeable*, I'd be honored if you could help me out to spread its message.

Here's a few ways you can help:

I would love your input to make the next version of this book (for the ladies!) and my future books better. Can you leave me a review on Amazon and let me (and the world) know what you thought? Your review will help a ton, trust me.

Share your copy with a friend. Or, anonymously text the Amazon link to them. Kidding, but seriously, the more people who start revamping their online dating presence and just as importantly, know *how to*, the better the dating world is for everyone.

WANT MORE CAMILA?

Bring her to your organization's next event, or to your local high school or college. Camila is an accomplished speaker who delivers talks and workshops around breaking stigmas in the areas of entrepreneurship, value alignment, mental health, immigration, and of course, dating (online and off!).

For more info, visit www.CamilaArriNudo.com

Made in the USA
Columbia, SC
12 October 2023

24356219R00039